The Blessings Of Obedience

The Blessings Of Obedience

Dr. FREDDY B. WILSON

The opinions expressed by the author are not necessarily those of
Wilsonet Enterprises
Originally published on Oct 28, 2014
Published by Wilsonet Enterprises
135 Bonnie Lane | Fayetteville, Georgia 30215 USA
404-754-0858 |
Wilsonet Enterprises is committed to excellence.
Book design copyright © 2017 by Wilsonet Enterprises. All rights
reserved.
Cover design by Dr. Freddy B. Wilson
Published in the United States of America
ISBN: 978-0-9987873-1-2
1. Religion / Christian Life / Personal Growth
2. Family And Relationship/General
17.05.08

Introduction

People use the word obedience often in the world today. Obedience in the worldly sense is important for republics like the United States of America that was built upon a set of laws that everyone is expected to obey. These societies expected people to obey the rules at their workplaces and expect children in families to obey the rules set by their parents. There are consequences to disobeying rules set in certain societies. There are also consequences when children do not follow the rules set by parents. The Bible discusses obedience in many different ways and verses.

Webster dictionary defines obedience as an act or instance of obeying. Webster defines obeying as "following the commands or guidance of". The Bible also provides examples of obedience and the blessings that follow obedience to God.

God subjected Abraham to an enormous trial of faith and obedience. God instructed Abraham to go to Mt. Moriah and offer up Abraham's son Isaac as a sacrifice. Abraham loved his son but did not question God. Human sacrifice probably already existed at that time so this would have been a certain loss to Abraham. Abraham decided to obey, because "he considered that God is able to raise men even from the dead" (Hebrews 11:19). Abraham built an altar and placed Isaac upon it. The Lord, seeing Abraham's faith, stopped him from killing Isaac.

God provided Abraham a ram caught in the thicket as a substitute for Isaac. It was no coincidence that the ram was caught in the thicket. When you obey God, He would have already provided provision for you once you fall under His Will. Abraham later called the place Jehovah-Jireh, "The Lord Will Provide." All promises formerly God made to Abraham were confirmed because of Abraham's obedience. God has a plan for you if and when you are ready to listen to His instruction.

Genesis 22:9 - 18 (NLT) [9]When they arrived at the place where God had told him to go, Abraham built an altar and arranged the wood on it. Then he tied his son, Isaac, and laid him on the altar on top of the wood. [10]And Abraham picked up the knife to kill his son as a sacrifice. [11]At that moment the angel of the LORD called to him from heaven, "Abraham! Abraham!" "Yes," Abraham replied. "Here I am!" [12]"Don't lay a hand on the boy!" the angel said. "Do not hurt him in any way, for now I know that you truly fear God. You have not withheld from me even your son, your only son." [13]Then Abraham looked up and saw a ram caught by its horns in a thicket. So he took the ram and sacrificed it as a burnt offering in place of his son. [14]Abraham named the place Yahweh-Yireh (which means "the LORD will provide"). To this day, people still use that name as a proverb: "On the mountain of the LORD it will be provided." [15]Then the angel of the LORD called again to Abraham from heaven. [16]"This is what the LORD says: Because you have obeyed me and have not withheld even your son, your only son, I swear by my own name that [17]I will certainly bless you. I will multiply your descendants beyond number, like the stars in the sky and the sand on the seashore. Your descendants will conquer the cities of their enemies. [18]And through your descendants all the nations of the earth will be blessed—all because you have obeyed me."

It Takes Faith to Be Obedient

It takes a considerable amount of faith in order to be obedient to God. It takes faith for it is not easy to follow the instructions of someone you have never seen before. You must have a close relationship to God to know His will for your life. Once God shows you what He wants you to do, you must do it faithfully without ever doubting what God is capable of doing. Do this no matter how foolish it may seem! Don't forget, God won't have you do anything that is against His Word. If you think God is telling to go commit a sin, such as adultery, then you'd better check and see who is talking to you, for it won't be God!

Hebrews 11:7 - 9 (NLT) [7]It was by faith that Noah built a large boat to save his family from the flood. He obeyed God, who warned him about things that had never happened before. By his faith Noah condemned the rest of the world, and he received the righteousness that comes by faith. [8]It was by faith that Abraham obeyed when God called him to leave home and go to another land that God would give him as his inheritance. He went without knowing where he was going. [9]And even when he reached the land God promised him, he lived there by faith—for he was like a foreigner, living in tents. And so did Isaac and Jacob, who inherited the same promise.

Having faith and staying in God's will goes beyond any religious act and religious rituals. One must have a personal relationship with God to hear clearly His voice when He is talking to you. People will hear many voices as they live their daily lives. In order to hear and clearly understand God's voice, a person must have a personal and "right" relationship with Him. There have been many instances in my life where I acted solely because God led me to do the act even though I had no clue as to what God was doing or where the act would lead me.

Romans 4:13 - 16 (NLT)
[13]Clearly, God's promise to give the whole earth to Abraham and his descendants was based not on his obedience to God's law, but on a right relationship with God that comes by faith. [14]If God's promise is only for those who obey the law, then faith is not necessary and the promise is pointless. [15]For

the law always brings punishment on those who try to obey it. (The only way to avoid breaking the law is to have no law to break!) [16]So the promise is received by faith. It is given as a free gift. And we are all certain to receive it, whether or not we live according to the law of Moses, if we have faith like Abraham's. For Abraham is the father of all who believe.

The Bible speaks of need for obedience in the book of Jeremiah.

Jeremiah 6:16 - 21 (NLT) [16] This is what the LORD says: "Stop at the crossroads and look around. Ask for the old, godly way, and walk in it. Travel its path, and you will find rest for your souls. But you reply, 'No, that's not the road we want!' [17] I posted watchmen over you who said, 'Listen for the sound of the alarm.' But you replied, 'No! We won't pay attention!' [18] "Therefore, listen to this, all you nations. Take note of my people's situation. [19] Listen, all the earth! I will bring disaster on my people. It is the fruit of their own schemes, because they refuse to listen to me. They have rejected my word. [20] There's no use offering me sweet frankincense from Sheba. Keep your fragrant calamus imported from distant lands! I will not accept your burnt offerings. Your sacrifices have no pleasing aroma for me." [21] Therefore, this is what the LORD says: "I will put obstacles in my people's path. Fathers and sons will both fall over them. Neighbors and friends will die together."

If you don't obey what God will have you do, there will be problems. You may not attribute your problem to your not obeying God but rest assure, God will allow things to happen just to get your attention! To go beyond mere obedience to God the Bible talks about a required relationship with God. A relationship with God is much different than simply believing in God and performing religious acts. Having a close relationship with God will allow you to communicate with Him and understand His will for you.

Jeremiah 7:1 - 26 (NLT) [1]The LORD gave another message to Jeremiah. He said, [2]"Go to the entrance of the LORD's Temple, and give this message to the people: 'O Judah, listen to this message from the LORD! Listen to it, all of you who worship here! [3]This is what the LORD of Heaven's Armies, the God of Israel, says: "'Even now, if you quit your evil ways, I will let you stay in your own land. [4]But don't be fooled by those who promise you safety simply because the LORD's Temple is here. They chant, "The LORD's Temple is here! The LORD's Temple is here!" [5]But I will be merciful only if you stop your evil thoughts and deeds and start treating each other with justice; [6]only if you stop exploiting foreigners, orphans, and widows; only if you stop your murdering; and only if you stop harming yourselves by worshiping idols. [7]Then I will let you stay in this land that I gave to your ancestors to keep forever. [8]"'Don't be fooled into thinking that you will never suffer because the Temple is here. It's a lie! [9]Do you really think you can steal, murder, commit adultery, lie, and burn incense to Baal and all those other new gods of yours, [10]and then come here and stand before me in my Temple and chant, "We are safe!"—only to go right back to all those evils again? [11]Don't you yourselves admit that this Temple, which bears my name, has become a den of thieves? Surely I see all the evil going on there. I, the LORD, have spoken! [12]"'Go now to the place at Shiloh where I once put the Tabernacle that bore my name. See what I did there because of all the wickedness of my people, the Israelites. [13]While you were doing these wicked things, says the LORD, I spoke to you about it repeatedly, but you would not listen. I called out to you, but you refused to answer. [14]So just as I destroyed Shiloh, I will now destroy this Temple that bears my name, this Temple that you trust in for help, this place that I gave to you and your ancestors. [15]And I will send you out of my sight into exile, just as I did your relatives, the people of Israel.' [16]"Pray no more for these people, Jeremiah. Do not weep or pray for them, and don't beg me to help them, for I will not listen to you. [17]Don't you see what they are doing throughout the towns of Judah and in the streets of Jerusalem? [18]No wonder I am so angry! Watch how the children gather wood and the fathers build sacrificial fires. See how the women knead dough and make cakes to offer to the Queen of Heaven. And they pour out liquid offerings to their other idol gods! [19]Am I the one they are hurting?" asks the LORD. "Most of all, they hurt themselves, to their own shame." [20]So this is what the Sovereign LORD says: "I will pour out my terrible fury on this place. Its people, animals, trees, and crops will be consumed by the unquenchable fire of my anger." [21]This is what the LORD of Heaven's Armies, the God of Israel, says: "Take your burnt offerings and your other sacrifices and eat them yourselves! [22]When I led your ancestors out of Egypt, it was not burnt offerings and sacrifices I wanted from them. [23]This is what I told them: 'Obey me, and I will be your God, and you will be my people. Do everything as I say, and all will be well!' ²⁴"But my people would not listen to me. They kept doing whatever they wanted, following the stubborn desires of their evil hearts. They went backward instead of forward. ²⁵From the day your ancestors left Egypt until now, I have continued to send my servants, the prophets—day in and day out. ²⁶But my people have not listened to me or even tried to hear. They have been stubborn and sinful—even worse than their ancestors.

This supports the fact that God wants you to be obedient at all times. God told the Israelites He was not looking for their offerings and sacrifices when He brought them out of Egypt but for them to listen Him and do as they were asked. He wanted to bless them. You don't have to understand everything God want you to do, but you must do what He tells you to do. Simply going to church and following rituals is not enough to be fully in God's will. Your relationship with him is quite important. Building this relationship will give you access to his riches by listening to and heeding his voice. If you follow God's guidance, you will never fail! Even in times of distress, obedience to God will help you prevail!

Luke 7:1 - 15 (NLT) [1]When Jesus had finished saying all this to the people, he returned to Capernaum. [2]At that time the highly valued slave of a Roman officer was sick and near death. [3]When the officer heard about Jesus, he sent some respected Jewish elders to ask him to come and heal his slave. [4]So they earnestly begged Jesus to help the man. "If anyone deserves your help, he does," they said, [5]"for he loves the Jewish people and even built a synagogue for us." [6]So Jesus went with them. But just before they arrived at the house, the officer sent some friends to say, "Lord, don't trouble yourself by coming to my home, for I am not worthy of such an honor. [7]I am not even worthy to come and meet you. Just say the word from where you are, and my servant will be healed. [8]I know this because I am under the authority of my superior officers, and I have authority over my soldiers. I only need to say, 'Go,' and they go, or 'Come,' and they come. And if I say to my slaves, 'Do this,' they do it." [9]When Jesus heard this, he was amazed. Turning to the crowd that was following him, he said, "I tell you, I haven't seen faith like this in all Israel!" [10]And when the officer's friends returned to his house, they found the slave completely healed. [11]Soon afterward Jesus went with his disciples to the village of Nain, and a large crowd followed him. [12]A funeral procession was coming out as he approached the village gate. The young man who had died was a widow's only son, and a large crowd from the village was with her. [13]When the Lord saw her, his heart overflowed with compassion. "Don't cry!" he said. [14]Then he walked over to the coffin and touched it, and the bearers stopped. "Young man," he said, "I tell you, get up." [15]Then the dead boy sat up and began to talk! And Jesus gave him back to his mother.

God Shows His Greatness Through Our Faith

God is good no matter what we are going through! We had family over from my wife's side who lost a young 29 year old mother. Unfortunately, the devil always wants to mess with you by creating arguments with family members. My wife and I ended up arguing over an issue with a family member. I didn't believe after all these years we have to deal with such stupid problems. As a couple, even though you don't always agree, you should have each other's back. Friendship in marriage is very important. Never do anything that will weaken your friendship with your spouse.

We as a couple experienced more discomfort being obedient to the Lord when my job reassigned me to Florida in November 2013. Things did not work out as planned so we decided in order for my wife to keep her new good-paying job, and for my girls to attend the high school they were in, I would have to move to Florida by myself, at least initially. While I realized I was doing the right thing by being obedient and making the move, the devil started working on my family. He first started making problems between my wife and daughters, then he tried to mess up things between my wife and me. This all happened after only being gone one week.

I know the promise of God and I had to clear my head and get back to not only asking God to keep my girls safe, but to also fix this problem. I am looking forward to God's showing me the real reason I came to Florida and working things out positively for my family.

In the Bible, God has instructed that we obey our "spiritual leaders". This, in my opinion, is not directing us to follow or live only by instruction of persons who designate themselves as "spiritual leaders". This does provide for us to follow instructions of those persons ordained by God to lead His people to a life that follows God's Word. Pastors, ministers, preachers and other spiritual leaders should be seen only as God's messengers. To keep this in perspective each person should have a personal relationship with God; therefore, our spiritual leaders will serve only as guides and advisors instead of being our only connection to God.

> **Hebrews 13:17 (NLT)** [17]Obey your spiritual leaders, and do what they say. Their work is to watch over your souls, and they are accountable to God. Give them reason to do this with joy and not with sorrow. That would certainly not be for your benefit.

A good spiritual leader will encourage their followers (or flock) to get a personal relationship with God for themselves. The leader's job is to guide and provide support to the people under his or her leadership. They should lead people to not just follow man-made rules and principles created by people at various churches but to discover and follow the Word of God. We must be willing to submit ourselves to God. We must be accountable to God day by day, and eventually at judgment. We must guard our thoughts and heart from lustful desires. We should always be willing to treat others with respect and kindness. Two things God expects of us all - love God and love people! How can you say you love God but hate or do evil things to the people God allows in our lives?

Matthew 12:36 - 37 (NLT) [36]And I tell you this, you must give an account on judgment day for every idle word you speak. [37]The words you say will either acquit you or condemn you."

Having faith is what God demands of us. We start our journey of obedience by first having faith in God. It's easy to say we are faithful when we already have a want or need. It is an entirely different thing to have faith that God will supply a want or need that is nowhere in sight. God's blessings are available to all who are faithful.

Romans 4:9 (NLT) [9]Now, is this blessing only for the Jews, or is it also for uncircumcised Gentiles? Well, we have been saying that Abraham was counted as righteous by God because of his faith.

When the world or your friends are watching you show your faith, be prepared to be ridiculed! Not everyone will understand your faith in God and some will even say you are crazy. That's a price we have to pay for our faith in God. You should not be taken aback about the things people say to you or about you due to your faith.

1 Peter 4:4 - 5 (NLT) [4]Of course, your former friends are surprised when you no longer plunge into the flood of wild and destructive things they do. So they slander you. [5]But remember that they will have to face God, who will judge everyone, both the living and the dead.

We are free moral agents and should entirely dependent upon our Creator for our existence. We are answerable to Him for our conduct. We owe Him our obedience and service. God has provided us His grace so we are without excuse if we fail to do God's will. Sometimes in doing God's will things won't go as you thought. This can be disturbing especially if you thought God led you to do a certain thing. I don't know everything about why God allows this to happen. I can say it can sometimes be part of a test to see if you willing to obey God. I can also say you should never doubt what God said he will do.

Leviticus 25:18 - 22 (NLT) [18]"If you want to live securely in the land, follow my decrees and obey my regulations. [19]Then the land will yield large crops, and you will eat your fill and live securely in it. [20]But you might ask, 'What will we eat during the seventh year, since we are not allowed to plant or harvest crops that year?' [21]Be assured that I will send my blessing for you in the sixth year, so the land will produce a crop large enough for three years. [22]When you plant your fields in the eighth year, you will still be eating from the large crop of the sixth year. In fact, you will still be eating from that large crop when the new crop is harvested in the ninth year.

The Lord told the people of Israel if they followed His laws that He would bless them with Palestine and its fertility. God instructed them to let the soil lie fallow in certain years. Therefore, when they placed its cultivation under obedience to the Lord's commands, it flourished.

God has instructed us to give to the poor. Because His instructions are clear, there is no reason for us not to be in His will. You will never lose when you follow God's plan for your life. You should seek out those who need you spiritually and occasionally, financially. When God tells you to give something (furniture, cars, money) to someone in need, you should not hesitate to do so. God will bless you with more than you gave.

Deuteronomy 15:4 - 6 (NLT)
[4]"There should be no poor among you, for the LORD your God will greatly bless you in the land he is giving you as a special possession. [5]You will receive this blessing if you are careful to obey

19

all the commands of the LORD your God that I am giving you today. [6]The LORD your God will bless you as he has promised. You will lend money to many nations but will never need to borrow. You will rule many nations, but they will not rule over you.

God will reward you even when the odds are against you. God blessed Amaziah with victory over the Edomites even though he was greatly out-numbered. Some of the enemies were destroyed without Amaziah having to lay hands on them. Ten thousand of them were dashed to pieces from the rocks of Sela.

The poverty level in Israel was not high since there was a willful distribution of property. They did this due to expected promised blessings from God as a result of their obedience. However, cases of need occasionally occurred. The book of Deuteronomy showed what Moses told the Israelites.

Deuteronomy 15:10 - 11 (NLT)
[10]Give generously to the poor, not grudgingly, for the LORD your God will bless you in everything you do. [11]There will always be some in the land who are poor.

That is why I am commanding you to share freely with the poor and with other Israelites in need.

The Call to Obedience

God demands obedience! While most of what we discuss here will be about obedience, an important thing to remember is that God has said he would punish any disobedience. God wants us to obey the commands He has set for all humankind.

---

2 Corinthians 10:3 - 6 (NLT)
[3]We are human, but we don't wage war as humans do. [4]We use God's mighty weapons, not worldly weapons, to knock down the strongholds of human reasoning and to destroy false arguments. [5]We destroy every proud obstacle that keeps people from knowing God. We capture their rebellious thoughts and teach them to obey Christ. [6]And after you have become fully obedient, we will punish everyone who remains disobedient.

Scripture require us to love everyone. If we obey this rule, it means that we are required to love even our enemies. However, I believe we are required to provide a special and warmer love for our brothers in Christ. This requires consideration of others in all we do and, sacrifice for others, and forgiveness. God will provide for the welfare of those who render Him obedience.

Exodus 24:1 - 3 (NLT) [1]Then the LORD instructed Moses: "Come up here to me, and bring along Aaron, Nadab, Abihu, and seventy of Israel's elders. All of you must worship from a distance. [2]Only Moses is allowed to come near to the LORD. The others must not come near, and none of the other people are allowed to climb up the mountain with him." [3]Then Moses went down to the people and repeated all the instructions and regulations the LORD had given him. All the people answered with one voice, "We will do everything the LORD has commanded."

There is much to gain in doing what God instructs you to do. There are benefits both seen and unseen. God will appoint His angels to watch over you even if you do not know they are there. God will have people move on your behalf even when they don't know why they are doing what they are doing and for whom it was being done.

Exodus 23:20 - 23 (NLT) [20]"See, I am sending an angel before you to protect you on your journey and lead you safely to the place I have prepared for you. [21]Pay close attention to him, and obey his instructions. Do not rebel against him, for he is my representative, and he will not forgive your rebellion. [22]But if you are careful to obey him, following all my instructions, then I will be an enemy to your enemies, and I will oppose those who oppose you. [23]For my angel will go before you and bring you into the land of the Amorites, Hittites, Perizzites, Canaanites, Hivites, and Jebusites, so you may live there. And I will destroy them completely.

God had a covenant with Israel. When the people accepted and honored the words of the Ten Commandments, God rewarded their obedience by providing constant care of Israel, victory over enemies, prosperity, and the pouring out of His Spirit. As long as they remained in God's will, God blessed them. When some of the people of Israel went outside of God's will, He punished them.

Every human being will face trials in life. God told us we are accountable for our actions and we should try to be good to others. God told us to abstain from all known evil. Not only are we to pray for ourselves but pray for others as well.

Job 42:7 - 10 (NLT) [7]After the LORD had finished speaking to Job, he said to Eliphaz the Temanite: "I am angry with you and your two friends, for you have not spoken accurately about me, as my servant Job has. [8]So take seven bulls and seven rams and go to my servant Job and offer a burnt offering for yourselves. My servant Job will pray for you, and I will accept his prayer on your behalf. I will not treat you as you deserve, for you have not spoken accurately about me, as my servant Job has." [9]So Eliphaz the Temanite, Bildad the Shuhite, and Zophar the Naamathite did as the LORD commanded them, and the LORD accepted Job's prayer. [10]When Job prayed for his friends, the LORD restored his fortunes. In

> fact, the LORD gave him twice as much as before!

These three men availed themselves to the intercession of Job in obedience to the divine command and God blessed them, including Job. Elijah is another example of God blessings for being obedient. Elijah fully submitted himself to God's will. His faith in God had no limit. He displayed full faith and courage even in times of trouble and danger, no matter who was present. His obedience was as unquestioning as that of a child's. How show compassion for those who were weak and the down-trotted. Elijah did not seek credit or publicity for his faith and trust in God. People of faith must show restraint, and involve self-denial for the sake of obedience. "For what will a man be profited, if he gains the whole world, and forfeits his soul?" (Matthew 16:26).

Not everyone is going to understand a faithful person who is willing to follow God's will for his or her lives. Some may think the person is crazy for stepping out and doing what God told them to do, you must be obedient to God no matter how impossible the task may seem.

Luke 2:41 - 52 (NLT) [41]Every year Jesus' parents went to

Jerusalem for the Passover festival. [42]When Jesus was twelve years old, they attended the festival as usual. [43]After the celebration was over, they started home to Nazareth, but Jesus stayed behind in Jerusalem. His parents didn't miss him at first, [44]because they assumed he was among the other travelers. But when he didn't show up that evening, they started looking for him among their relatives and friends. [45]When they couldn't find him, they went back to Jerusalem to search for him there. [46]Three days later they finally discovered him in the Temple, sitting among the religious teachers, listening to them and asking questions. [47]All who heard him were amazed at his understanding and his answers. [48]His parents didn't know what to think. "Son," his mother said to him, "why have you done this to us? Your father and I have been frantic, searching for you everywhere." [49]"But why did you need to search?" he asked. "Didn't you know that I must be in my Father's house?" [50]But they didn't understand what he meant. [51]Then he returned to Nazareth with them and was obedient to them. And his mother stored all these things in her heart. [52]Jesus grew in wisdom and in stature and in favor with God and all the people.

The Rewards

Being obedient to God's Word will come with much reward. Elijah was fed by being obedient. God told him something to do and he did it even though he probably did not understand why God told him to go where God instructed him. We must do the same in our lives. God speaks to us and we must be quiet enough to hear Him.

Hebrews 1:1 - 2 (NLT) [1]Long ago God spoke many times and in many ways to our ancestors through the prophets. [2]And now in these final days, he has spoken to us through his Son. God promised everything to the Son as an inheritance, and through the Son he created the universe.

A recent example in my life of being blessed by obedience was with a situation I found myself in with my vehicle loans. In 2011, I went against my common sense and out of love for my eldest daughter I co-signed on a car loan to help her build her credit. My credit at that time was good but not where it used to be. As a result of my daughter's credit being so bad I had to accept a higher interest rate than what I would ever have accepted. Not only that, I ended up being the primary on the vehicle (a 2010 Toyota Camry) and she was secondary. I essentially financed the car in my name for her use. Additionally and shortly after buying my daughter the Camry, by praying and having faith in God, I was able to buy a car I had wanted for a while, a 2009 Smart Car.

My daughter initially kept up with the payments but got behind later. She managed to get caught up but later fell behind again. Out of trying to help her again, I told her I could come and get the car. This would make her eligible to get another car for we were so upside down ($7,000) it would hurt her to try to trade it for something cheaper. After I caught a bus from Georgia to Florida and picked up the car, my daughter later offered to get the car payments caught up if I brought it back to her. I prayed about it and realized that I had done the right thing by going to get the car. My wife and I wondered how I would be able to make the payments on the car along with our other pressing bills. I told her I didn't know but since I was following God's word, I knew He would make a way. I prayed that I would never personally have to make a payment on the high-interest loan on my daughter's car. I planned on trading the car in for a lower interest payment.

I went to 6 different car dealerships trying to make a deal. The balance owed on the car had gone from $18,000 to over $19,000. The first blessing was that I worked with the finance company and they agreed to me making make-up payments as I paid the regular payment and they would report them as being on time. I still looked for opportunities to trade in my daughter's Camry. I was repeatedly turned down for loans due to my now low credit score and how much I was upside down. I even tried to trade my daughter's old car and my Smart Car in to reduce my insurance and amount of payments. I dealt with a Lexus dealership that finally was able to say they think they could get me approved but it was at a higher interest rate than what I was paying for my daughter's car.

As I was getting closer to when the agreed to payments were due on the Camry, the Lord told me to go back to the Lexus dealership. I told God that He knew the deal had not been formally approved and the interest rate was too high. God told me to go back anyway and I would be blessed. After some contact with them they agreed to give me $1000 more for the Camry than what other dealerships offered. This dealership was on the opposite side of town from where I lived and God blessed me to work it out to have both cars on that dealership's side of town at the same time.

When I went to see the business manager, after some conversation he offered to work with the bank but the best he could do would lower the interest by 2%. That still would have been 2% higher than the interest on the Camry. After realizing that this would still be a blessing considering between the two cars I was $10,000 upside down but I knew the Lord had something better. After it was all said and done, right before I had to sign the contract, the Lord blessed me to where the interest had been lowered by 4.5%! This made the deal low enough to enable me to now afford to buy an extended warranty on the new car.

Some reading this will only look at the debt I was entering but this sort of blessing goes way beyond common understanding of finances. When you do what God will have you do you cannot fail! You might have to go through some things along the way that you don't understand.

---

1 Kings 17:1 - 7 (NLT) [1]Now Elijah, who was from Tishbe in Gilead, told King Ahab, "As surely as the LORD, the God of Israel, lives—the God I serve— there will be no dew or rain during the next few years until I give the word!" [2]Then the LORD said to Elijah, [3]"Go to the east and hide by Kerith Brook, near where it enters the Jordan River. [4]Drink from the brook and eat what the ravens bring you, for I have commanded them to bring you food." [5]So Elijah did as the LORD told him and camped beside Kerith Brook, east of the Jordan. [6]The ravens brought him bread and meat each morning and evening, and he drank from the brook. [7]But after a while the brook dried up, for there was no rainfall anywhere in the land.

This is also an example of God doing what He said He would do if we are obedient. God told Elijah to go and warned him there would be a drought. The drought occurred just as God had warned. Sometimes God will push us out of our comfort zones in order to bless us. Sometimes we chose to remain where we are or with the wrong persons because that is what we are used to. This could be out of fear of just plain stubbornness. Occasionally we can get confused as to which way the Lord is leading us. We must remain in prayer and God will lead us.

---

2 Corinthians 2:9 - 10 (NLT) [9]I wrote to you as I did to test you and see if you would fully comply with my instructions. [10]When you forgive this man, I forgive him, too. And when I forgive whatever needs to be forgiven, I do so with Christ's authority for your benefit,

33

In order to have obedience there must be order. God has established His expectations of order in the world as well as in families. The Bible teaches us that the father is the head of the household. He has the obligation of bringing up his children in the fear of God. The father is supposed to get his children well acquainted with Biblical law, respect for authority and being a mentor. Moses enforced duty and obedience to both parents (Exodus 20:12). During those times, any outrage against parents was a capital offense.

Deuteronomy 21:18 - 21 (NLT)
[18]"Suppose a man has a stubborn and rebellious son who will not obey his father or mother, even though they discipline him. [19]In such a case, the father and mother must take the son to the elders as they hold court at the town gate. [20]The parents must say to the elders, 'This son of ours is stubborn and rebellious and refuses to obey. He is a glutton and a drunkard.' [21]Then all the men of his town must stone him to death. In this way, you will purge this evil from among you, and all Israel will hear about it and be afraid.

The Bible spoke of the advantages and benefits to obeying parents.

Ephesians 6:1 - 3 (NLT)
[1]Children, obey your parents because you belong to the Lord, for this is the right thing to do. [2]"Honor your father and mother." This is the first commandment with a promise: [3]If you honor your father and mother, "things will go well for you, and you will have a long life on the earth."

In all this, God still established boundaries on parents. God expects children to obey their parents but He did not want parents to take unfair advantage of this privilege by allowing abuse to come in.

Colossians 3:20 - 21 (NLT)
[20]Children, always obey your parents, for this pleases the Lord. [21]Fathers, do not aggravate

your children, or they will become discouraged.

The moral teaching of Christianity had a significant bearing on the relationship between master and servants. This relationship can be transferred today to the relationship between employer and employee and between any relationships between an average person to one in authority. God expects obedience, reverence, and gratefulness.

---

1 Timothy 5:3 - 4 (NLT) [3]Take care of any widow who has no one else to care for her. [4]But if she has children or grandchildren, their first responsibility is to show godliness at home and repay their parents by taking care of them. This is something that pleases God.

God can bless the servant to become the one over the person who was once master or the person once in charge. You do not always have to view the person in authority as the enemy but God said He would make your enemy your footstool. This does not always mean that the person who was once the servant will become the master, although it could happen. It can also mean that God will use that person in authority to become a blessing to the subordinate, whether the person (or leader) wants to do it or not.

Exodus 12:35 - 36 (NLT) [35]And the people of Israel did as Moses had instructed; they asked the Egyptians for clothing and articles of silver and gold. [36]The LORD caused the Egyptians to look favorably on the Israelites, and they gave the Israelites whatever they asked for. So they stripped the Egyptians of their wealth!

Deuteronomy 6:17 - 19 (NLT) [17]You must diligently obey the commands of the LORD your God—all the laws and decrees he has given you. [18]Do what is right and good in the LORD's sight, so all will go well with you. Then you will enter and occupy the good land that the LORD swore to give your ancestors. [19]You will drive out all the enemies living in the land, just as the LORD said you would.

Following God's instructions

Once in obedience, God will expand your horizons! He will provide for you and enable you to accomplish things beyond your wildest imagination. God will not only make you a fisherman, capable of feeding and providing for your family, but He will make you a fisher of men. Through your example and actions, God will enable you to show others to Him.

Luke 5:1 - 7 (NLT) [1]One day as Jesus was preaching on the shore of the Sea of Galilee, great crowds pressed in on him to listen to the word of God. [2]He noticed two empty boats at the water's edge, for the fishermen had left them and were washing their nets. [3]Stepping into one of the boats, Jesus asked Simon, its owner, to push it out into the water. So he sat in the boat and taught the crowds from there. [4]When he had finished speaking, he said to Simon, "Now go out where it is deeper, and let down your nets to catch some fish." [5]"Master," Simon replied, "we worked hard all last night and didn't catch a thing. But if you say so, I'll let the nets down again." [6]And this time their nets were so full of fish they began to tear! [7]A shout for help brought their partners in the other boat, and soon both boats were filled with fish and on the verge of sinking.

Jesus expects obedience when He calls you for a purpose. James and his brother were fishermen and were partnered with Simon Peter (Luke 5:10). When Jesus called James and his brother to be his followers they responded with unquestioned obedience. Things will be a little simpler for us if we just obey what God tells us to do. He will never lead us astray.

Mark 1:16 - 20 (NLT) [16]One day as Jesus was walking along the shore of the Sea of Galilee, he saw Simon and his brother Andrew throwing a net into the water, for they fished for a living. [17]Jesus called out to them, "Come, follow me, and I will show you how to fish for people!" [18]And they left their nets at once and followed him. [19]A little farther up the shore Jesus saw Zebedee's sons, James and John, in a boat repairing their nets. [20]He called them at once, and they also followed him, leaving their father, Zebedee, in the boat with the hired men.

Once again, not everyone will heed the call from the Lord to serve. Many who do answer the call do not fully follow God's laws and precepts, not understanding the full blessing of obeying God. When you do answer God's call not everyone will understand what you are doing and why. They will later wonder how you are able to be as blessed and/or as confident as you are. Confidence comes from knowing the Lord and knowing He will bless you, regardless of your circumstances, but in His own time.

The prophet Ahijah acted in confidence for he knew that if he obeyed God's, God would grant him a kingdom equal to David's kingdom. Ahijah knew there was a price to pay or sacrifices necessary to follow Christ. Today, believers must be willing to give up much of their selves in order to obey the Lord.

---

1 Kings 11:29 - 39 (NLT) [29]One day as Jeroboam was leaving Jerusalem, the prophet Ahijah from Shiloh met him along the way. Ahijah was wearing a new cloak. The two of them were alone in a field, [30]and Ahijah took hold of the new cloak he was wearing and tore it into twelve pieces. [31]Then he said to Jeroboam, "Take ten of these pieces, for this is what the LORD, the God of Israel, says: 'I am about to tear the kingdom from the hand of Solomon, and I will give ten of the tribes to you! [32]But I will leave him one tribe for the sake of my servant David and for the sake of Jerusalem, which I have chosen out of all the tribes of Israel. [33]For Solomon has abandoned me and worshiped Ashtoreth, the goddess of the Sidonians; Chemosh, the god of Moab; and Molech, the god of the Ammonites. He has not followed my ways and done what is pleasing in my sight. He has not obeyed my decrees and regulations as David his father did. [34]"But I will not take the entire kingdom from Solomon at this time. For the sake of my servant David, the one whom I chose and who obeyed my commands and decrees, I will keep Solomon as leader for the rest of his life. [35]But I will take the kingdom away from his son and give ten of the tribes to you. [36]His son will have one tribe so that the descendants of David my servant will continue to reign, shining like a lamp in Jerusalem, the city I have chosen to be the place for my name. [37]And I will place you on the throne of Israel, and you will rule over all that your heart desires. [38]If you listen to what I tell you and follow my ways and do whatever I consider to be right, and if you obey my decrees and commands, as my servant David did, then I will always be with you. I will establish an enduring dynasty for you as I did for David, and I will give Israel to you. [39]Because of Solomon's sin I will punish the descendants of David—though not forever.'"

We must be wise and seek the Lord in all we do. We need to stop relying solely on man-made systems we have grown to rely on. This includes our intelligence, our education, our connections, our associations, our money, the influence we have gained on our jobs or in communities, and even credit scores. I am not saying any of these are bad things to have but sometimes we give them more credence than we do credit to The Lord. Having the right kind of wisdom will lead us away from depending on ourselves or these systems.

Proverbs 8:1 - 5 (NLT) [1] Listen as Wisdom calls out! Hear as understanding raises her voice! [2] On the hilltop along the road, she takes her stand at the crossroads. [3] By the gates at the entrance to the town, on the road leading in, she cries aloud, [4] "I call to you, to all of you! I raise my voice to all people. [5] You simple people, use good judgment. You foolish people, show some understanding.

Matthew 16:24 - 27 (NLT) [24]Then Jesus said to his disciples, "If any of you wants to be my follower, you must turn from your selfish ways, take up your cross, and follow me. [25]If you try to hang on to your life, you will lose it. But if you give up your life for my sake, you will save it. [26]And what do you benefit if you gain the whole world but lose your own soul? Is anything worth more than your soul? ²⁷For the Son of Man will come with his angels in the glory of his Father and will judge all people according to their deeds.

Our relationship with God will lead us to bright futures if we do what God will have us do. Having a personal relationship with God will enable us to discern the voice of God. Do not turn your ear to instruction. God placed in us some of our internal desires and passions so take heed to where he leads you.

Proverbs 13:13 - 15 (NLT)
¹³ People who despise advice are asking for trouble; those who respect a command will succeed. ¹⁴ The instruction of the wise is like a life-giving fountain; those who accept it avoid the snares of death. ¹⁵ A person with good sense is respected; a treacherous person is headed for destruction.

An example of following instructions was when Jesus attended a wedding.

John 2:1 - 10 (NLT) [1]The next day there was a wedding celebration in the village of Cana in Galilee. Jesus' mother was there, [2] and Jesus and his disciples were also invited to the celebration. [3]The wine supply ran out during the festivities, so Jesus' mother told him, "They have no more wine." [4]"Dear woman, that's not our problem," Jesus replied. "My time has not yet come." [5]But his mother told the servants, "Do whatever he tells you." [6]Standing nearby were six stone water jars, used for Jewish ceremonial washing. Each could hold twenty to thirty gallons. [7]Jesus told the servants, "Fill the jars with water." When the jars had been filled, [8]he said, "Now dip some out, and take it to the master of ceremonies." So the servants followed his instructions. [9]When the master of ceremonies tasted the water that was now wine, not knowing where it had come from (though, of course, the servants knew), he called the bridegroom over. [10]"A host always serves the best wine first," he said. "Then, when everyone has had a lot to drink, he brings out the less expensive wine. But you have kept the best until now!"

Jesus' mother was faithful enough to know that Jesus could do anything He wanted and she instructed the servants to do what He told them. The servants followed instructions as directed and witnessed a miracle. In the midst of your problems God can bless you in ways you never thought of in your prayers.

John 9:1 - 7 (NLT) [1]As Jesus was walking along, he saw a man who had been blind from birth. [2]"Rabbi," his disciples asked him, "why was this man born blind? Was it because of his own sins or his parents' sins?" [3]"It was not because of his sins or his parents' sins," Jesus answered. "This happened so the power of God could be seen in him. [4]We must quickly carry out the tasks assigned us by the one who sent us. The night is coming, and then no one can work. [5]But while I am here in the world, I am the light of the world." [6]Then he spit on the ground, made mud with the saliva, and spread the mud over the blind man's eyes. [7]He told him, "Go wash yourself in the pool of Siloam" (Siloam means "sent"). So the man went and washed and came back seeing!

This means it takes more than just having faith to stay in God's will. It also takes being obedient enough to do what you are told and not question God. This might mean doing something you are uncomfortable with or you do not fully understand why you are doing it. Understand also that God will never tell you to do evil. You must act on faith!

Matthew 17:14 - 20 (NLT) [14]At the foot of the mountain, a large crowd was waiting for them. A man came and knelt before Jesus and said, [15]"Lord, have mercy on my son. He has seizures and suffers terribly. He often falls into the fire or into the water. [16]So I brought him to your disciples, but they couldn't heal him." [17]Jesus replied, "You faithless and corrupt people! How long must I be with you? How long must I put up with you? Bring the boy to me." [18]Then Jesus rebuked the demon in the boy, and it left him. From that moment the boy was well. [19]Afterward the disciples asked Jesus privately, "Why couldn't we cast out that demon?" [20]"You don't have enough faith," Jesus told them. "I tell you the truth, if you had faith even as small as a mustard seed, you could say to this mountain, 'Move from here to there,' and it would move. Nothing would be impossible."

As mentioned previously, there is a blessing in following instruction. Some people think obedience is belittling, not so! Passages in Deuteronomy show us that if we do what the Lord says, we will be blessed.

Deuteronomy 28:1 - 8 (NLT) [1]"If you fully obey the LORD your God and carefully keep all his commands that I am giving you today, the LORD your God will set you high above all the nations of the world. [2]You will experience all these blessings if you obey the LORD your God: [3] Your towns and your fields will be blessed. [4] Your children and your crops will be blessed. The offspring of your herds and flocks will be blessed. [5] Your fruit baskets and breadboards will be blessed. [6] Wherever you go and whatever you do, you will be blessed. [7]"The LORD will conquer your enemies when they attack you. They will attack you from one direction, but they will scatter from you in seven! [8]"The LORD will guarantee a blessing on everything you do and will fill your storehouses with grain. The LORD your God will bless you in the land he is giving you."

You must follow Godly instruction even if you do not understand why God would have you do a specific thing. Jesus' disciples in Matthew obeyed even if they did not understand why Jesus had them do what He instructed.

Working Through the Confusion of Following God's Will

One of the hardest things to do as a believer is to take a step you think to be foolish but at the same time know God told you to trust Him and do it. I experienced some delays in writing this book for due to other things not going the way I thought they should, I wondered if I should continue to write. I took steps that I knew God wanted me to do only to later feel I made a mistake for I experienced difficulty along the way. It took me a while to realize that although I had experience personal difficulty, God was there for me all along!

In the summer of 2013 my job went through a reorganization which left me with an assignment to relocate to Tampa, FL. At first I thought this was a problem for when I moved back to Atlanta, I thought I would never have to move again. As it relates to the job, God put situations in place to let me realize I was being blessed. On the other hand, there were four things I had to deal with in having to buy a new house in Florida. The first was my twin daughters were just going to the 11th grade and wanted to be with their friends. I eventually got them to realize we would have to move. The second was my wife had just got a new job that she really loved and it could lead to a career. My wife had followed me in my military and civilian career and sacrificed a lot. She was an at-home mom for quite a while then doing menial and service jobs outside the home to help out. When she got situated in a good job, we

51

moved again and now I did not want to mess that up for her.

The next problem was my 18 year old daughter had graduated that year and had not gone to college yet. She wanted attend a school in Atlanta and now we were moving. That meant she would have to move to an apartment for the school she was interested in did not have dorms. At that time we did not have the means to put her in an apartment.

The last problem is the one I felt God would bless me past. God showed me some nice houses that I felt he would bless me to provide for my family. Most of the houses were beyond what I could finance based on my job but I know that through faith, God can bless you beyond your credit score. When I went to Tampa, FL to work on the future permanent job located I contacted a realtor about started to look at houses. Before we got started I told him I wanted to see what my bank would finance. I had already gone out to two of the communities I was interested and liked the areas I had chosen. The problem came when they came back with my credit score and they told me it probably would not be approved based on the circumstances.

Although I knew God is the god of all circumstances, I was floored! I said, Lord, how can this be? I still knew God would bless me but I am also aware of how the rest of the world operates. Some realtors only want to show you homes you are qualified to buy. God had wakened me earlier that morning telling me He was going to bless me but now I was wondering how. God told me to just pay attention and I would know what to do. I paid attention and now wondered should I wait on The Lord to bless me to pay off my house in Atlanta and still buy a house in Tampa or did it mean I should rent a place in Tampa for me only for now and let my family remain in our home in Atlanta.

Although it hurt me to feel that I did something God told me and found myself disappointed, I still knew I must do what God told me. In the past I did things I know The Lord told me to do and they didn't work out but eventually after keeping on listening to Him, things worked out better than they would have if the blessing came when I first tried. I think God tests us sometimes just to see if we would obey. I know God will work this thing out for me!

In the midst of having to make a decision regarding possibly moving my family, I lost my older brother (eldest child in the family). I loved my brother and this event took a bigger toll on me than I expected. I lived around the corner from my brother and his family. Now I had to wonder at a time like this should sell my house which would keep my family close to my brother's family so my family could be there for them if they need anything. Through sad thoughts of losing my brother, praying for his family, and now wondering what to do with my family, I began to wonder why God hadn't shown me clearly what I should do regarding if I should sell my home or lease it out and rent a house in Tampa. The other option would be to keep them in place, fight through the problems of being separated from my family, or buy an RV to live in Tampa instead of being in an apartment.

At one point I became frustrated that God had not told me clearly which way to go as he did when I bought my house in Fayetteville, GA. I do know that if God is in a decision you make, there is always peace in the decision and God will provide all the provisions in whatever direction you go.

Matthew 21:1 - 6 (NLT) [1]As Jesus and the disciples approached Jerusalem, they came to the town of Bethphage on the Mount of Olives. Jesus sent two of them on ahead. [2]"Go into the village over there," he said. "As soon as you enter it, you will see a donkey tied there, with its colt beside it. Untie them and bring them to me. [3]If anyone asks what you are doing, just say, 'The Lord needs them,' and he will immediately let you take them." [4]This took place to fulfill the prophecy that said, [5] "Tell the people of Israel, 'Look, your King is coming to you. He is humble, riding on a donkey— riding on a donkey's colt.'" [6]The

> two disciples did as Jesus commanded.

One thing you must understand is that not all the God will have you do is about you! God may have you do a certain thing to be a blessing to someone else or to prepare for an event that God will usher in.

Author Joyce Armster said Webster's dictionary defines being obedient as being submissive to the restraint or command of authority: willing means to obey with joy. Isn't it amazing that we want our children to be obedient to us, and we get furious if they don't? Well, God wants us to be obedient to him to. Isaiah 1:19 says, "if ye be willing and obedient, ye shall eat the good of the land" (NLT).

Armster said we forget that obedience must be learned. Obedience to the commandments of God seems to be one of man's most difficult challenges. Some people do not obey because they feel their free agency will be trampled upon. They justify their course of action by shrugging and saying, "That's just the way I am". Armster said one goal that most of us share in this life is the desire to achieve true joy and lasting happiness. There is only one way to do this, and that is by being obedient to all the commandments of God.

The Ten Commandments were given so that all could see the extent of their failure to obey God's laws (see Romans 5:1-21). Armster said keeping the commandments of God is not a difficult burden when we do it out of love of Him who has so graciously blessed us. The most difficult part of obeying God's law is simply deciding to start now.

Armster wrote that obedience challenges us to go beyond mere understanding. If you don't obey God when he speaks to you, you are essentially saying, "God, I don't trust Your will for my life". I don't think You have my best interest at heart. I know better than You, so I will handle this one myself.

Armster expounded by writing obedience challenges us to go beyond mere outward conformity – God judges our hearts as well as our deeds, for it is in the heart that our real allegiance lies. Be just as concerned about your attitudes that people do not see as about your actions seen by all. Obedience challenges us to act out of love for God – Jesus was saying that his listeners needed a different kind of righteousness altogether (love and obedience). Our righteousness must (1) come from what God does in us, not what we can do by ourselves (2) be God-centered, not self-centered (3) go beyond keeping the law to living by the principles behind the law.

Armster encouraged us by writing that obedience brings about a change, such as disciplining our lives in all things – one process by which we can discipline ourselves is by repentance, for it "is the way to annul the effects of a previous lack of obedience in one's life.

Armster wrote that there are benefits that we can expect from God when we are obedient to God. Obedience to God keeps us from harm – If you will listen to the voice of the Lord your God, and obey it, and do what is right, then I will not make you suffer the diseases I sent on the Egyptians, for I am the Lord who heals you. (Exodus 15:26) Obedience to God is pleasing to Him –to be successful, follow God's words in Joshua 1:8. You may not succeed by the world's standards, but you will be a success in God's eyes—and his opinion lasts forever. Obedience to God often leads to peace – obedience may not always bring peace with our enemies, but it will bring peace with God.

Armster said all believers should know that obedience is part of the Christian experience. Job 5:17 says, Blessed is the man whom God corrects. As long as you are obedient to God He will bless you. In your obedience, you will be blessed, but as with all of God's promises, there is a prerequisite. YOU MUST OBEY!

What About Disobedience?

The Bible speaks of the blessings of obedience in Leviticus 26.

Leviticus 26:1-13 [1]"Do not make idols or set up carved images, or sacred pillars, or sculptured stones in your land so you may worship them. I am the LORD your God. [2]You must keep my Sabbath days of rest and show reverence for my sanctuary. I am the LORD. [3]"If you follow my decrees and are careful to obey my commands, [4]I will send you the seasonal rains. The land will then yield its crops, and the trees of the field will produce their fruit. [5]Your threshing season will overlap with the grape harvest, and your grape harvest will overlap with the season of planting grain. You will eat your fill and live securely in your own land.

[6]"I will give you peace in the land, and you will be able to sleep with no cause for fear. I will rid the land of wild animals and keep your enemies out of your land. [7]In fact,

you will chase down your enemies and slaughter them with your swords. [8]Five of you will chase a hundred, and a hundred of you will chase ten thousand! All your enemies will fall beneath your sword. [9]"I will look favorably upon you, making you fertile and multiplying your people. And I will fulfill my covenant with you. [10]You will have such a surplus of crops that you will need to clear out the old grain to make room for the new harvest! [11]I will live among you, and I will not despise you. [12]I will walk among you; I will be your God, and you will be my people. [13]I am the LORD your God, who brought you out of the land of Egypt so you would no longer be their slaves. I broke the yoke of slavery from your neck so you can walk with your heads held high.

Although not the focus of this book, Leviticus also spoke on the punishments for disobedience.

Leviticus 26:14-20 [14]"However, if you do not listen to me or obey all these commands, [15]and if you break my covenant by rejecting my decrees, treating my regulations with contempt, and refusing to obey my commands, [16]I will punish you. I will bring sudden terrors upon you—wasting diseases and burning fevers that will cause your eyes to fail and your life to ebb away. You will plant your crops in vain because your enemies will eat them. [17]I will turn against you, and you will be defeated by your enemies. Those who hate you will rule over you, and you will run even when no one is chasing you! [18]"And if, in spite of all this, you still disobey me, I will punish you seven times over for your sins. [19]I will break your proud spirit by making the skies as unyielding as iron and the earth as hard as bronze. [20]All your work will be for nothing, for your land will yield no crops, and your trees will bear no fruit.

The Bible also speaks of disobedience in Deuteronomy. The Bible mentioned a person could be cursed for disobeying God. I think some of my blessings were delayed for doing things I knew God didn't want me to do. I must admit that at times in my life I didn't do something for thinking I'd be better off doing something else or allowing other people or other things distract me from what I should be doing. That was one of my concerns when I faced decision about what to do with my family in 2014 and losing my brother. I wondered if there was something I was supposed to be doing that I had not.

Hebrews 4:11 (NLT) [11]So let us do our best to enter that rest. But if we disobey God, as the people of Israel did, we will fall.

The bible spoke of curses for disobedience:

Deuteronomy 28:15 - 20 (NLT) [15]"But if you refuse to listen to the LORD your God and do not obey all the commands and decrees I am giving you today, all these curses will come and overwhelm you: [16] Your towns and your fields will be cursed. [17] Your fruit baskets and breadboards will be cursed. [18] Your children and your crops will be cursed. The offspring of your herds and flocks will be cursed. [19] Wherever you go and whatever you do, you will be cursed. [20]"The LORD himself will send on you curses, confusion, and frustration in everything you do, until at last you are completely destroyed for doing evil and abandoning me.

Don't get caught up in greed as you live your life. We often look for something in return for our obedience. Rewards will come but that should not be your sole reason for obedience. Obey God out of love and reverence.

Colossians 3:5 - 6 (NLT) [5]So put to death the sinful, earthly things lurking within you. Have nothing to do with sexual immorality, impurity, lust, and evil desires. Don't be greedy, for a greedy person is an idolater, worshiping the things of this world. [6]Because of these sins, the anger of God is coming.

Although Moses presented to Israel the Ten Commandments, obeying God is much simpler than following a set of rules. Simply put, God calls for us to love and obey Him.

Deuteronomy 10:12-16 [12]"And now, Israel, what does the LORD your God require of you? He requires only that you fear the LORD your God, and live in a way that pleases him, and love him and serve him with all your heart and soul. [13]And you must always obey the LORD's commands and decrees that I am giving you today for your own good.

[14]"Look, the highest heavens and the earth and everything in it all belong to the LORD your God. [15]Yet the LORD chose your ancestors as the objects of his love. And he chose you, their descendants, above all other nations, as is evident

today. [16]Therefore, change your hearts and stop being stubborn.

Deuteronomy 11:8-15

[8]"Therefore, be careful to obey every command I am giving you today, so you may have strength to go in and take over the land you are about to enter. [9]If you obey, you will enjoy a long life in the land the LORD swore to give to your ancestors and to you, their descendants—a land flowing with milk and honey! [10]For the land you are about to enter and take over is not like the land of Egypt from which you came, where you planted your seed and made irrigation ditches with your foot as in a vegetable garden. [11]Rather, the land you will soon take over is a land of hills and valleys with plenty of rain—[12]a land that the LORD your God cares for. He watches over it through each season of the year! [13]"If you carefully obey all the commands I am giving you today, and if you love the LORD your God and

serve him with all your heart and soul, [14]then he will send the rains in their proper seasons—the early and late rains—so you can bring in your harvests of grain, new wine, and olive oil. [15]He will give you lush pastureland for your livestock, and you yourselves will have all you want to eat.

We sometimes think we have to understand everything before we do what God tells us. This could lead us to be deceived, either by ourselves or through others. We need to only trust God for direction in our lives and remain true to Him through faith. We must show this faith in our lives. Don't be ashamed of your faithfulness in God. Don't be ashamed and place your relationship with God aside to fit in with others or to prove you are not different than them. As my former pastor, Pastor Rodney Akins of Jonesboro, GA often said, we are a peculiar people. Peculiar does mean different but that difference should not be considered a negative difference. Being a peculiar people places us in a better predicament than others. We should seek the Lord's approval and not that of other people.

Deuteronomy 11:16-21 [16]"But be careful. Don't let your heart be deceived so that you turn away from the LORD and serve and worship other gods. [17]If you do, the LORD's anger will burn against you. He will shut up the sky and hold back the rain, and the ground will fail to produce its harvests. Then you will quickly die in that good land the LORD is giving you. [18]"So commit yourselves wholeheartedly to these words of mine. Tie them to your hands and wear them on your forehead as reminders. [19]Teach them to your children. Talk about them when you are at home and when you are on the road, when you are going to bed and when you are getting up. [20]Write them on the doorposts of your house and on your gates, [21]so that as long as the sky remains above the earth, you and your children may flourish in the land the LORD swore to give your ancestors.

When you trust in the Lord, obey His commands, and stay in His will, the Bible discusses a myriad of blessings you can expect from the Lord. These blessings are by-products of your relationship and faith in God. You should not do things for the kingdom of God with an earthly reward in mind. God should be revered just for being who he is and not only for what he can do for you.

Deuteronomy 28:1-9 [1]"If you fully obey the LORD your God and carefully keep all his commands that I am giving you today, the LORD your God will set you high above all the nations of the world. [2]You will experience all these blessings if you obey the LORD your God:

[3] Your towns and your fields will be blessed.

[4] Your children and your crops will be blessed. The offspring of your herds and flocks will be blessed.

[5] Your fruit baskets and breadboards will be blessed.

[6] Wherever you go and whatever you do, you will be blessed.

[7]"The LORD will conquer your enemies when they attack you.

They will attack you from one direction, but they will scatter from you in seven!

[8]"The LORD will guarantee a blessing on everything you do and will fill your storehouses with grain. The LORD your God will bless you in the land he is giving you.

[9]"If you obey the commands of the LORD your God and walk in his ways, the LORD will establish you as his holy people as he swore he would do. [10]Then all the nations of the world will see that you are a people claimed by the LORD, and they will stand in awe of you.

Stay in God's Will

When you stay in the Lord's will and completely trust Him, you don't have to be overly concerned about your life's future. God will never leave you alone.

At the beginning of June 2013, my organization went through reorganization. We had expected my current boss to take the leadership position that was created at my location. Our higher headquarters decided to give the position to someone else. That created a problem since even though they were going to bring the new boss to my location, they did not create another personnel position for him to fill. We would have four people filling three authorized positions. This meant one of the people at my location would have to move. Higher headquarters decided I would have to move since I have been on station the longest (at that time 6-1/2 years). This was the longest I have been at any one location since I started doing this job.

During a previous conversation with my current boss I told him that if I ever had to move, I would like to be considered for placement in Fort Walton Beach, FL (where my wife is from) or Tampa, FL (where my eldest daughter and grandchild lived). I don't know why I told him that for at that time they said I would not have to worry about moving again since they were trying to create stability for our organization's civilians.

By the second week of June 2013, my boss told me they were planning on relocating me to Tampa, FL to fill a leadership position in a small unit. At first I was appalled they wanted me to move! God had blessed my family with a wonderful house in Fayetteville, GA, in a great community with good schools, and I did not want to give it up. Then I realized that although going to something new was unpleasant, I was being offered a location that I had asked for. That in itself was a blessing!

I then became concerned about all it would take to sell our current home and the hassle of buying another one. If I bought a house like ours in Fayetteville, GA in Tampa, FL, it would cost me almost $1,000,000. There were other circumstances that I was aware that would make it difficult for me to purchase another home. I had to do some reflection. Gospel singer, Tye Tribbett, sings a song that says, "If He did it before, He can do it again." This is so true. I did not have any money when God told me to buy the current house my family lives in. In 2006, God made a way for me to buy the Fayetteville house and then sell the old Williamsburg, VA house at the price we asked.

Sometimes we as Christians will tell the Lord, "Wherever you want me to go, send me". But when the Lord tries to send us to some new place we balk and question what's going on. I had to go into prayer and say to the Lord that if my job was moving me, and it was not in His will, to cut it off. If God wanted me to go, then He would make a way for everything and I didn't have to worry. My family and I will be blessed with another nice home and God will show me what to do with our current home. One thing I learned along the way is that when God blesses you with something nice you don't have to hang on to it for believe it or not, God can bless you with something nicer!

Deuteronomy 28:11-14 [11]"The LORD will give you prosperity in the land he swore to your ancestors to give you, blessing you with many children, numerous livestock, and abundant crops. [12]The LORD will send rain at the proper time from his rich treasury in the heavens and will bless all the work you do. You will lend to many nations, but you will never need to borrow from them. [13]If you listen to these commands of the LORD your God that I am giving you today, and if you carefully obey them, the LORD will make you the head and not the tail, and you will always be on top and never at the bottom. [14]You must not turn away from any of the commands I am giving you today, nor follow after other gods and worship them.

When you follow in God's will, remember not to act on your own understanding and go beyond the purpose of God wanted you to do. Don't do anything unless you have asked God about it. This is why it is so important to have a close relationship with the Lord. We sometimes want to be like God and do things only because we assumed it would please God. In the Bible, the Lord rejects Saul when he thought he was doing what would please the Lord.

---

1 Sam 15:20-23 [20]"But I did obey the LORD," Saul insisted. "I carried out the mission he gave me. I brought back King Agag, but I destroyed everyone else. [21]Then my troops brought in the best of the sheep, goats, cattle, and plunder to sacrifice to the LORD your God in Gilgal." [22]But Samuel replied, "What is more pleasing to the LORD: your burnt offerings and sacrifices or your obedience to his voice? Listen! Obedience is better than sacrifice, and submission is better than offering the fat of rams. [23] Rebellion is as sinful as witchcraft, and stubbornness as bad as worshiping idols. So because you have rejected the command of the LORD, he has rejected you as king."

You must be willing to go do what the Lord will have you do. Ask the Lord to lead you.

Philippians 2:4 - 8 (NLT) [4]Don't look out only for your own interests, but take an interest in others, too. [5]You must have the same attitude that Christ Jesus had. [6] Though he was God, he did not think of equality with God as something to cling to. [7] Instead, he gave up his divine privileges; he took the humble position of a slave and was born as a human being. When he appeared in human form, [8] he humbled himself in obedience to God and died a criminal's death on a cross.

I briefly mentioned earlier about how God blessed my family in 2006 to buy house in Fayetteville, GA. That is a classic example of how God can bless you if you simply stay in His will. The rest of the story was I was not even in the market to buy a house. My mother had been sick in 2005 and God placed it in my heart to want to move back to the Atlanta area. After talking to the doctors I realized my mother would probably not be able to live alone as she had been. I wanted to get a house big enough for my mother to move in with my family.

Philippians 2:17 (NLT) [17]But I will rejoice even if I lose my life, pouring it out like a liquid offering to God, just like your faithful service is an offering to God. And I want all of you to share that joy.

On my last visit to Atlanta I went alone without my family and stayed with my brother and his family in Fayetteville, GA. As I was leaving their house there was a house being built around the corner from my brother's house that caught my attention. Please understand there were other new houses being built in the neighborhood and I drove past this one on my way into the neighborhood and never previously noticed it. Something told me to turn into the driveway and take a look. I asked God, why? I am not in the market to buy a house, especially since my job was in Virginia.

I said, OK Lord, I'm listening so I got out to look at the house. Now I know it was God talking to me when he told me to take my camera with me. The house was primary in frame and I couldn't tell what the house was going to look like. There were two men on the property when I showed up. One was the realtor and the other was the builder. When I talked to the realtor I accidentally as questions like, how many bedrooms does my house have? How far back does my property go? When I apologized for my verbal missteps by calling it my house, the realtor said to not worry for it could be my house.

I found out the house wasn't intended to be for sale, it was going to be my builder's model home for it was the first one he was building in that community. I told them I was interested in buying the house but had to consult with my wife. When I left there I called my wife and told her what God had showed me. To my surprise and without having seen the house, my wife agreed with me. I still could not fully understand why God placed it on my heart to buy this house. Especially since I did not have a job in the Atlanta area, nor did I have the money.

As I was driving back to Virginia that day after looking at the house and talking to my wife, I got this strange phone call from my office. They told me I had been selected to deploy to Afghanistan. Then I realized the reason God was having me move to Georgia. My wife told me when we first went to Virginia that she did not want to be there and the only reason she was there was to be with me and keep the family together. She said at the beginning that she would only stay in Virginia three years. God knew that if I deployed to Afghanistan with my wife still in Virginia, we probably would have divorced and went our separate ways.

There still was an issue with my not having a job in Atlanta that would enable me to move there. I told the Lord I would be obedient and I knew He would make a way. Unfortunately, my mother passed away in October 2005. My wife and family visited the house later and we looked at other houses being built in the new neighborhood. Although we all liked the house God showed me, there were others in the neighborhood that were more complete or completed and were also less expensive. I told my family that God showed me the one house and I was not interested in the others, although I liked some of them.

We decided we would try to buy the new house. Barring the problem with not having a job in Atlanta, we also did not have earnest money to put down in trying to buy the house. As we prayed in the access road driveway, I told my family if this was God acting, then there would be something in the mail when we get back to Virginia that would take care of that problem. Sure enough, there was a check in the mail when we returned. Now on to the next problem: selling our house in Virginia.

To make a long story short, we went through a lot of mess and had to listen to a lot of nay-sayers when we tried to sell our house in Virginia. The developer had at least three brand-new homes available for sale in our neighborhood so other neighbors told us we would not be able to sell our home. This was also during the time the housing market was slowing down and during normal winter slowdown. We had one family that kept low-balling the price and on each offer they wanted more of our personal property, such as our custom built, 70 gallon fish aquarium made in the Philippines. After a while, although it appeared we were desperate, I told our realtor we would not entertain any more offers from this family for at that point I knew God would make a way regardless of the market and other situations.

We put a contract on the house in Fayetteville, GA but it was completed before we sold our house in Williamsburg, VA. We needed the equity from the old house in order to purchase the new home. At least, that was the world's way of buying a new house. It seemed our prayers were not answered when a closing date in January 2006 came and went and we were not able to close due to not selling our old house. As the family was praying together one night, I stopped and said, wait a minute. I told God we would no longer tie His hands by asking to sell our old house in order to buy the new one. We would not wait for Him to show how he would make a way for this to happen.

The first blessing came when we were referred to this short-term lending company. I know some of you will wonder how I will consider this a blessing. Keep reading. We were approved for a first mortgage for the main house loan, and a second mortgage for what would have been our down payment. We were able to close on the house in February 2006. I told my wife and anyone that would listen that if this was God, which I knew it was, then I would never have to make a payment of these high interest loans.

Although my family had moved into our new house in Fayetteville, GA I had to return to Williamsburg, VA to an empty house that we were waiting to sell. The next blessing came with a family who liked the additions we made to the house, the well-manicured yard, and a nice refrigerator who paid the asking price on our home! By the time we went to closing on the old house, I had one day for the payment due on the new house's high interest mortgages, I paid them off without having to make any payments as I discussed previously. I forgot to mention we went from managing a first and second mortgage on the old house, and the first and second mortgage on the new house, to one lower interest mortgage on the new house. This was done just in time for me to deploy to Afghanistan. God is so good!

The last blessing came during the time I was serving honorably in Afghanistan. For dutifully deploying to Afghanistan and working hard there, my commander approved an assignment for me relocate to the Atlanta area within months of my return for overseas. The extra money earned in Afghanistan helped us take care of things needed for the new house, including paying to complete our basement. Isn't God amazing? This all came as a result of my being obedient with what God told me.

Psalms 143:8 - 10 (NLT) [8] Let me hear of your unfailing love each morning, for I am trusting you. Show me where to walk, for I give myself to you. [9] Rescue me from my enemies, LORD; I run to you to hide me. [10] Teach me to do your will, for you are my God. May your gracious Spirit lead me forward on a firm footing.

You Must Have a Personal Relationship with God

Having a personal relationship with God will enable you to listen to His directions for your life.

> **2 Chronicles 27:6** ⁶King Jotham became powerful because he was careful to live in obedience to the LORD his God.

As God is blessing you there must be reverence to what He has done and will do for you. You cannot forget from whom your blessings come. Continued obedience to the Lord will save your life. The people of Israel at some point lost their obedience to the Lord.

> **Ezekiel 20:13** ¹³"But the people of Israel rebelled against me, and they refused to obey my decrees there in the wilderness. They wouldn't obey my regulations even though obedience would have given them life."

You should not be ashamed to tell others about your obedience to the Lord. However, when you are walking in God's light you have to be a shining example of being Godly. Although you are not expected to be perfect, you must show wisdom and righteousness in all you do.

When people see your blessings, they only see what you have and don't know what you went through to get where you are. I have heard somewhere the best way to get a blessing is to be a blessing to someone else. At one point in our lives, God had blessed us with three vehicles, a full sized SUV for the family, a commuter car for me, and an older (but nicely equipped) mini-van. I loved that min-van and had paid to add some nice electronics such as a mobile entertainment system for the kids. My sister-in-law had been experiencing financial struggle taking care of her two kids by herself and had bad luck with vehicles that would break down. I was out of town one day on business and God put it on my heart to bless my sister-in-law with the mini-van free of charge. I was initially shocked that God would have me give up something I loved but I knew I had to be obedient. My next hurdle was what my wife would think of what I thought compelled to do.

I used the direct approach and told my wife what God told me to do. The van was still worth about $8,000 and I thought my wife would have a fit, especially since the van was paid for. To my surprise, my wife did not object to my plan. We called my sister-in-law and told her what we were going to do. She was shocked! She said she could use the mini-van and offered to pay us something on it. We told her to consider it a gift from God and we did not want any money from her. We gave her a bill of sale and signed the title over to her. I knew somewhere along the way God would bless us for being obedient.

> **Romans 16:19-20** [19]For your obedience has become known to all. Therefore I am glad on your behalf; but I want you to be wise in what is good, and simple concerning evil. [20]And the God of peace will crush Satan under your feet shortly.

You don't have to be the most eloquent speaker when God calls you to speak for Him. There are many stories told in the Bible where all the receiver of the message had to do was be obedient enough to do what God tells him to do. I discovered my talent is writing. I plan on writing for the Lord. In 2012 I was called on to speak at a gathering. I am not afraid to talk in front of people but I never thought I would be called upon for this kind of speaking. The truth is God prepared me for this event and it went well! I have been called to speak on a panel on two more occasions since then. We have to learn to call on the blood of Jesus to make us whole.

The truth about the blood is that it has everlasting power!

Acts 8:26 - 35 (NLT) [26]As for Philip, an angel of the Lord said to him, "Go south down the desert road that runs from Jerusalem to Gaza." [27]So he started out, and he met the treasurer of Ethiopia, a eunuch of great authority under the Kandake, the queen of Ethiopia. The eunuch had gone to Jerusalem to worship, [28]and he was now returning. Seated in his carriage, he was reading aloud from the book of the prophet Isaiah. [29]The Holy Spirit said to Philip, "Go over and walk along beside the carriage." [30]Philip ran over and heard the man reading from the prophet Isaiah. Philip asked, "Do you understand what you are reading?" [31]The man replied, "How can I, unless someone instructs me?" And he urged Philip to come up into the carriage and sit with him. [32]The passage of Scripture he had been reading was

> this: "He was led like a sheep to the slaughter. And as a lamb is silent before the shearers, he did not open his mouth. [33] He was humiliated and received no justice. Who can speak of his descendants? For his life was taken from the earth." [34]The eunuch asked Philip, "Tell me, was the prophet talking about himself or someone else?" [35]So beginning with this same Scripture, Philip told him the Good News about Jesus.

Should we just obey what the Lord would have us do, we can be so blessed! Sometimes things seem impossible but if God put us up to it, he will guide us through.

Don't think for a minute that just because you're doing what God will have you do, that things are going to be easy. You have to watch what you tell folks along the way for there are people out there that would work to prove you wrong.

An example of this is when the government decided to move my family and I out of San Antonio 3 years after I became a civilian agent. I did not want to leave our lovely home in our wonderful community.

We had installed an above ground pool that the whole family loved. After much prayer, the Lord told me to not fight the move for we will be blessed on the next assignment. We hired a realtor that I told that God was going to bless us to sell our home. This realtor seemed to do nothing for us in helping to sell our home. The only person we knew him to bring to our home to show came on the day he knew we were moving out! Boxes were all over the place! The house did not sell under regular means but since I was a civilian the government had to buy my house under an approved relocation program. I think the realtor was out to prove the house would not sell for he questioned me about what I said about what God had shown me. We were truly blessed on our next house.

Do not be afraid of the unknown when God tells you to do something. In Gen: 46:3, God told Jacob to not be afraid to go to Egypt. God promised blessings there for when he arrived.

During the so-called Tough Economic Times (TEC) and in the year 2010, I was perplexed for I was concerned about the amount of gas my wife was using in our large family SUV for work and our business. We were putting gas in the truck every four days and having to fill a 27 gallon tank was costly. We had two luxury cars already that were not fit to do the job (they were other blessings) and our son had a small car we could not use because of his school schedule and it also did not fit the bill. I was looking at a new Ford Transit Connect (a small enclosed truck) that would fit the bill but we did not the one with the back seats I wanted and they were outside of what I wanted to pay in cost and monthly payments. I went online and found a small truck at a local Toyota Dealership but it had no bells and whistles but it was priced around $2k less that it was work and it had low miles. I did not understand why they were selling the truck at such a low price but who am I to question this. I was also concerned for I had recently tried to buy another vehicle and the people told me I had too many cars financed already. By conventional wisdom, I should not have been in the market to buy yet another vehicle (this would be our 5th car on our insurance). The Lord told me not to be afraid and go ahead and check out the truck. I drove the truck and found it to be a very nice truck but it had none of the luxury features we were used to. This truck had manual windows, manual locks, and a manual transmission. It was a short bed and my research showed it got between 22-28 miles to the gallon. When I called my wife with what I had she said the truck would fit our needs. I again was hesitant for I wondered if I could afford the truck. Again, God told me not to worry about it. I completed the application and they told me we had to put my wife on as primary and they too asked the questions about why we had so many vehicles. I told them this truck would be used for our business. We took the truck home but I wondered if the underwriters would reject the deal as it had happened in the past. When God is going to bless you, you cannot go by what has happened to you in the past.

God will provide you with whatever you need if you stay in his will! I later found out the deal was approved and our payment was only $263 per month. The difference is putting gas in our SUV compared to the little truck saved us in the long run. God knew what he was doing! Furthermore, after again listening to God tell me He wanted me to cut loose from a certain group and I obeyed; we received an email message from a business contact who put us in touch with someone needing their building cleaned. God blessed us with more work that would help pay for the new truck. God is so good!

The story of Joshua shows the power of obedience. Joshua meditated on God's word day and night. Joshua had to lead the Israelites after Moses wasn't able to make it to the promise land.

Joshua 1:6 - 9 (NLT) [6]"Be strong and courageous, for you are the one who will lead these people to possess all the land I swore to their ancestors I would give them. [7]Be strong and very courageous. Be careful to obey all the instructions Moses gave you. Do not deviate from them, turning either to the right or to the left. Then you will be successful in everything you do. [8]Study this Book of Instruction continually. Meditate on it day and night so you will be sure to obey everything written in it. Only then will you prosper and succeed in all you do. [9]This is my command—be strong and courageous! Do not be afraid or discouraged. For the LORD your God is with you wherever you go."

Joshua is a prime example of how blessed you can be by following the Word of God. Most of our problems are that we are more concerned about pleasing people than we are about pleasing God. People don't want to lose friendships and relationships with other people. Those same people can't do for us as God can. We must be married to the purpose of God, make decisions regardless of who else understands.

I want to discuss how we were blessed with two Lexus cars when there was confusion to buy one (statement). Joel Olsten once said the problem is us not dreaming big enough (Delays sermon). When I returned from deployment from Afghanistan in 2006, my family was already living in our house in Atlanta while I was waiting being reassigned to Atlanta. I was considering replacing my 2004 Toyota Prius with a Camry Hybrid to get rid of the road noise I was experiencing. I loved my Prius but I knew I was ready for something better. I had prayed about what I should do. I ended up seeing an updated version of the Prius that I considered buying. I prayed while I was on the lot and God spoke to me and told me He would bless me with something better. I didn't know what that meant but I left the lot knowing I was not going to buy a newer Prius.

One night after I left Bible study, I went by a different Toyota dealership and looked at some new Camry Hybrids. I just did not get a feel for buying the car. Just as I was leaving, God spoke to me and told me to go by the Lexus dealership. I went by the Lexus dealership on my way home and saw a beautiful 2007 Lexus ES350 that was a special color called Ruby Red. I thought, wow, my wife will love this car. We had gone the dealership a long time ago when the model was an ES330 and she liked the Candy Apple Red. The dealership was closed so I decided to call a salesman I knew there the next day.

When I called the salesman the next day he explained to me that car arrived the night I saw it and the only reason it was there was because a customer had ordered it at another dealership and changed their mind and her dealer swapped it with my dealer for another color. He said that color was normally only special ordered and if I was interested I'd better come down that day. I went to the dealership on my way home from work. The salesman and I were inside talking and then walked outside to look at what was purposed to be my wife's car. As I stepped out the door I walked by a silver 2007 Lexus GS450h, a sporty Hybrid 6-cylinder car that put out as much horse power as car with a V8 engine.

I fell in love! I asked the salesman about that car and he asked me if I wanted to drive it. I should have never driven the car for I really liked it! We went back to the dealership and talked about the cars. Now I wanted to buy the silver car for myself. I told the salesman I had to leave and think about what I needed to do. I went and sat in a grocery store parking lot and asked The Lord what I shall do. I could not believe how much this thing ad me wondering what I was doing and how I was going to do it. The silver car was much more expensive than any car I had ever purchased. The end of the story was that God told me not to be afraid of being blessed. I was approved to purchase the silver car for myself. I felt bad that I went to buy my wife a car (unbeknownst to her) and I purchased one for myself. I picked up my car on a Friday or Saturday. As I was sleeping in my hotel room late the Saturday night (early Sunday morning), about 3:30 and The Lord awakened me and told me to go back and buy the red car for my wife. I asked God, what?! I just barely got approved to buy my car and wondered how in the world I would be approved to pay for the second car? I did what God told me to do.

I went down to the dealership later on Sunday after church. The car was still there but the dealership was closed. I called the salesman on Monday. He said the car was still there but there was a lot of interest in the car, especially due to its color. When I was down there later that day, a salesman came up to get the keys to let someone else test drive the car, I grabbed the keys and told him no, this car was sold (the loan had not been officially approved yet but I acted on faith). Through God, the loan was approved and I then had to work on getting the cars from Virginia to Georgia to surprise my wife. Due to other financially foolish things my wife and I had to deal with (credit cards, etc), there were times we had trouble making the payments but God told me not to let them go. At the time of my writing this story, I only have 5 months to pay them both off! This is what obedience can do for you. I am not materialistic by any means but God knows that I like cars and motorcycles and saw fit to bless us with nice cars. God may have blessed us as a result of being obedient previously by giving away a vehicle to someone in need.

There was a time when we needed money to pay off a problematic bill. I went to a bank to apply for a loan and was declined. I then went to a few other banks trying to get the same loan and was declined as well. I earnestly was trying to work with this creditor but they were being difficult to work with. I prayed to God what I should do when I knew God was going to bless me but nothing seemed to be working in my favor. I was down on my knees often praying that God would deliver my family and I from this problem. One day I had prayed and was talking to The Lord about what I should do. God told me to go back to the first bank that had denied me. It was clear to me what God told me to do but I told God, "but they turned me down before". Even though I was feeling bad about having to go back to that same bank again, I did what God told me to do. Guess what, I was approved for the loan! I must say I was quite surprised for it didn't make sense to me to go back to a bank that had previously told me no. I used the money to pay the problematic bill and successfully paid the loan off. We as Christians must realize God has the power to change the hearts and minds of people. Learn to discern the voice of God and do as He tells you.

---

1 Kings 17:8 - 16 (NLT) [8]Then the LORD said to Elijah, [9]"Go and live in the village of Zarephath, near the city of Sidon. I have instructed a widow there to feed you." [10]So he went to Zarephath. As he arrived at the gates of the village, he saw a widow gathering sticks, and he asked her, "Would you please bring me a little water in a cup?" [11]As she was going to get it, he called to her, "Bring me a bite of bread, too." [12]But she said, "I swear by the LORD your God that I don't have a single piece of bread in the house. And I have only a handful of flour left in the jar and a little cooking oil in the bottom of the jug. I was just gathering a few sticks to cook this last meal, and then my son and I will die." ¹³But Elijah said to her, "Don't be afraid! Go ahead and do just what you've said, but make a little bread for me first. Then use what's left to prepare a meal for yourself and your son. ¹⁴For this is what the LORD, the God of Israel, says: There will always be flour and olive oil left in your containers until the time when the LORD sends rain and the crops grow again!" ¹⁵So she did as Elijah said, and she and Elijah and her son continued to eat for many days. ¹⁶There was always enough flour and olive oil left in the containers, just as the LORD had promised through Elijah.

Trust in God

One of the hardest things we as believers to do is trust God with our money. We may say we trust him around fellow Christians but we do a different thing when it comes to our acts or in how we give to the church. Many of us only go by what we see. The widow that served Elijah is a good example of when we are blessed by having faith and trusting in what God will have us do.

In August 2013 I was dealing with the fact my job wanted to move me from the Atlanta, GA area to Tampa, FL. I was not happy about it at first but managed to later realize that God had something special for me. This was hard for me for I thought I would retire in our current home that God blessed us with; to which my family and I really love. I talked to friends, family, and my pastor about my dilemma and finally realized I should only trust God. Although you may love a certain thing, such as a car or house or city, don't distress should God want you to move on to something else. I am already expecting something better than I have now. No, better does not necessarily mean bigger but I am willing to accept whatever blessings God has for me and my family.

I know it can be confusing when someone else is directing you in how to be blessed financially through faith. Those persons are useful in helping you find the faith and trust in God that you need; however, I must revert to saying that your blessing is dependent upon your relationship with God and whether you are able to hear and abide by what He tells you.

For example, I can tell you that God told me to tell you to put $100 in church today and you will be blessed. First, rest assure, I would never tell you something like that unless I thought God told me to tell you. Second, when you hear something like this you should be able to ask God on your own what He wants you to do. Then you can make your own decision as to what to do.

There are some true prophetic voices out there that are truly inspirational but you must be able to discern what applies to you.

---

1 Timothy 4:12 - 13 (NLT)
[12]Don't let anyone think less of you because you are young. Be an example to all believers in what you say, in the way you live, in your love, your faith, and your purity. [13]Until I get there, focus on reading the Scriptures to the church, encouraging the believers, and teaching them.

Conclusion

You have to seek God's will for your life and not let others keep you from being all you can be under God's direction. You just may be the answer to your family's prayers if you just get yourself in order and follow God's plan for your life.

---

1 Chronicles 21:18 - 19 (NLT)
[18]Then the angel of the LORD told Gad to instruct David to go up and build an altar to the LORD on the threshing floor of Araunah the Jebusite. [19]So David went up to do what the LORD had commanded him through Gad.

Because of their sin and David's disobedience, God punished the people of Israel. God sent David a message through a prophet and David decided to obey God's instructions. His actions saved the people of Israel and God ceased his punishment after David obeyed. I am here to tell you that you can't go wrong by following the Word and Will of God! The fact that I wrote this book is but one example of my being obedient to what the Lord tells me to do.